BROTHERS AND SISTERS

glimpses of the cloistered life

BROTHERS AND SISTERS

glimpses of the cloistered life

Frank Monaco

FOREWORD BY RON HANSEN

MARLOWE & COMPANY
NEW YORK

"Bernard, Bernard, why have you come here?"

the Abbot of Clairvaux often asked himself during his novitiate,

and to this replied:

"To hide myself in the face of the Lord".

✢ ✢ ✢

Dedicated to Brothers and Sisters, everywhere

BROTHERS AND SISTERS: GLIMPSES OF THE CLOISTERED LIFE

Text and Photographs copyright © 2001 by Frank Monaco
Foreword copyright © 2001 by Ron Hansen
Design copyright © 2001 Four Seasons Publishing Ltd

Published in the North America by
MARLOWE & COMPANY
An Imprint of Avalon Publishing Group Incorporated
161 William Street, 16th Floor
New York, NY 10038

Library of Congress Catalog Control Number 2001089217

ISBN 1-56924-578-9

9 8 7 6 5 4 3 2 1

Designed in association with
THE BRIDGEWATER BOOK COMPANY
Photographs printed by Albert Boulton

Printed in Singapore
Distributed by Publishers Group West

Foreword

by Ron Hansen

✛   ✛   ✛

CLOSE TO THE MIDDLE of Frank Monaco's glorious *Brothers and Sisters* there is a photograph of a professed sister pinning the snow white veil of a novice on a smiling college-age woman who seems to have just shorn off all her hair. The soft light, the parade behind them of gray gothic archways, and the harmony and simplicity of the composition help to suggest an undiscovered painting by the Dutch master Jan Vermeer. Underneath it is a quotation from St. Teresa of Ávila's sixteenth-century Carmelite handbook, *Way of Perfection*, that is essential to our understanding of monasticism's attractiveness: 'Oh, Sisters, for the love of God, try to realize what a great favour the Lord has bestowed on us whom he has brought here.'

Love and favour. The happiness that men and women find in consecrated, cloistered life is what surprises outsiders most. When, on his journey to Asia, the Cistercian priest and writer Thomas Merton had a private meeting with the Dalai Lama, a frustrated man listening at the door reported that all he could hear was continuous laughter. And on my occasional visits to monasteries the lasting impression I have is of happening upon monks in unexpected moments of mirth.

Ascetic religious life in the twenty-first century would seem to be so lacking in pleasure and allure that only fools and masochists would choose it. And indeed the talent and temperament for such a way to holiness seems to be quite rare. But in the silence of enclosure, in the rhythm and orderliness of routine, the elimination of the distractions and attachments of wealth, the abiding constraints of obedience and boundaries, and in the selfless and otherworldly focus of the life, the soul is at liberty, the spirit is given wings.

Enclosed religious communities fulfill Christ's command to pray without ceasing through the Liturgy of the Hours, a choir recital of hymns, psalms, and biblical or hagiographical readings, that supplies the architecture of their daily existence. Even today, the life of conventual monks and nuns is regulated by a schedule of activities that is fairly similar to that of the Cistercians as Thomas Merton portrayed it fifty years ago in *The Waters of Siloe*:

A.M.

2:00 Rise, go to choir, recite Matins and Lauds of Our Lady's Office.

2:30 Meditation.

3:00 Night Office, which features the canonical hours of Matins and Lauds.

4:00 Priests say their private Masses, others go to

Communion. Then there is time for reading or private prayer.

5:30 The hour of Prime, followed by Chapter, which is a community meeting, and possibly a light breakfast (or *frustulum*) of coffee, bread, and occasionally a hard-boiled egg.

6:30 Reading, study, or private prayer.

7:45 The hour of Tierce, High Mass, and the hour of Sext.

9:00 Work or study.

10:45 Reading or prayer.

11:07 None, the fifth of the seven canonical hours.

11:30 The primary meal, consisting of soup, fresh fruit, a side dish of cooked vegetables, bread, and coffee.

P.M.

12:15 Reading or private prayer.

1:30 Work.

3:30 Reading or private prayer.

4:30 The hour of Vespers.

5:15 Meditation.

5:30 Collation, which is some bread, a little fruit, and a hot drink.

5:40 Reading, prayer.

6:10 The hour of Compline, the hymn *Salve Regina*, and examination of conscience.

7:00 All go to bed.

Ora et labora, pray and work, was the essence of the Rule of St. Benedict, the sixth century code that provides the fundamental structure for all the religious congregations featured in *Brothers and Sisters*. But a good many photographs in this book also illustrate just how central to monastic culture is reading and the life of the mind; for the sanctuary of cloister is the perfection of a spiritual and intellectual environment for seeking, discerning, intimating, adoring, and resting in the presence of Mystery.

The sisters and brothers in the pages that follow are signs of contradiction. They have found love in celibacy, freedom in discipline, quest in stability, hungers satisfied in a regimen of fasting, needs met in poverty, fulfillment in selflessness, and conversation with the Holy One in elected silence.

✢   ✢   ✢

Ron Hansen is the author of numerous books, including the novels Mariette in Ecstasy *and* Atticus.

Preface

by Frank Monaco

✤　✤　✤

AS A PHOTO-JOURNALIST for an American magazine, the first monastery I ever visited was outside Serra San Bruno in Southern Italy. Erected in 1094 by St. Bruno, founder of the Carthusian Order, it was destroyed in the 1783 earthquake and later rebuilt.

The approach to its isolated situation was posted by a sign-board marked, '*O Bonitas*' ('O Goodness'). St. Bruno, it was said, saw goodness existing everywhere... in you, in me, in everything.

Inside the monastery gate, within view of the earthquake ruins of a chapel, I was ushered before the Prior. After a check of my credentials, I was invited to stay and given permission, with restrictions, to take photographs.

The life of the Carthusian monk is known for its discipline and solitude. And as photographs of them were rare, my magazine made excellent use of them and a set of prints sent to the Prior in return for their hospitality was warmly acknowledged.

That was the start of my monastic file of photographs, and later, as I was allowed through the gates of Benedictine, Cistercian and Franciscan monasteries, pictures were added to the file... pictures intended to record, '*O Bonitas*'.

After my photographic book on the monastic life of monks was published, the aim was to produce a similar book on the cloistered lives of nuns. With the blessing and permission of the Papal See, an approach to one convent brought this reply from the Abbess...

'The Sisters might possibly give a grudging assent to some photographs of the house, and even to one or other Sister as long as she remained "faceless". I'm quite sure some Sisters would hide completely if they thought they were going to be photographed. Although I feel slightly impatient at this attitude, nevertheless I feel I could not impose this on them.'

Eventually, with time and patience, I was invited into the convents of the Benedictines, the Carmelites and the Poor Clares – an environment where men are almost entirely forbidden – for a glimpse of the lives of those women who had chosen to devote themselves wholly to the service of the Lord.

A visitor is usually permitted to stay in a monastery for three days. There seems to be a traditional reckoning to this time. In the medieval past, it was assumed that three days were required to make an impression on the intellectual, emotional and instinctive nature of a visitor. However, to cover the activities of the monks, un-restricted time was given. And I was permitted to spend forty-two days among the nuns.

During that time with the nuns, there was a moment that will always remain with me; it took place among the Poor Clares. One evening when their meal was over, and Grace had been recited, a Poor Clare kneeled before the Abbess and said, 'I confess my fault to God and to you, Mother Abbess, and all the sisters, for all the faults and negligences I have committed and all the bad example and pain I have given you. I humbly ask you to forgive me and to ask Our Lord to be merciful to me and give me the grace to renew my vows with greater love and fervour than I have ever done before.' She then embraced each sister, saying, 'God reward you, dear Sister, for your grace and patience. I humbly ask for further patience.' This ceremony happens for each nun on the eve of the anniversary of her taking the vows.

Not long after the picture-taking among the nuns was over, I began to put together a portfolio of prints for each convent in gratitude for their hospitality. While viewing the pictures, there was one in particular that caught and held my attention. It was of a nun in full-length view, cleaning a window in the chapel. For some obscure reason, not sure of what I was looking for, I started to search through my file of monastic monks. And there it was... a picture of a monk in full-length view, cleaning a window in a cloister!

Further searching revealed the side-by-side engagement that existed between monk and nun in the cell, novitiate, worship, labour, meals and recreation. They were engaged in the religious life like a family... like Brothers and Sisters.

✛   ✛   ✛

The Monk

by Frank Monaco

✧   ✧   ✧

ABOUT SEVENTEEN HUNDRED YEARS AGO, an Egyptian youth, Anthony, gave his possessions away when his parents died and turned to a religious life. After years of solitude in the desert, the stories of his holiness drew people to settle as hermits on the site of his primitive hermitage. When, one day, St. Anthony was called upon to preach to the community, it was the beginning of Christian monasticism. Two hundred years later St. Benedict's rule, with its 73 chapters of common sense and moderation, established the ideal for Western monasticism.

Today, as then, once the thoughts of a man become concerned with God, he may seek unity with Him through prayer and detachment. According to his nature, he may be drawn to cut himself off from the world and its earthly attractions and one day, his desire for union with God may draw him to the monastic life, where he will enter as a postulant.

The postulant's introduction to his new life is conducted by the Master of Novices, an experienced monk, 'skilled in winning souls' (St. Benedict). By watching, the Master of Novices will learn about the physical, intellectual and psychic capacities of his charge. He will be on the alert 'to eliminate those subjects for whom our way of life, with its silence and solitude, is not suitable – those with difficult characters, or who lack docility; those who attract attention by singularity, by a tendency to melancholy, or the like' (Usages of the Cistercian Monks).

The period before a novice takes his final vows varies with each order. The novitiate in the Carthusian Order can take eight years – six of them will have been spent in the study of Latin, philosophy and theology – while the Benedictine monk will have spent almost five years as a novice. The novice is entirely free to depart from the community at any point until he takes his final vows.

During all the intervening centuries since St. Benedict's first foundation, the triple vows of the monk – poverty, chastity and obedience – have remained unchanged. Denying himself wealth, wife and will, he surrenders himself to the Abbot. Holding the place of Christ in the community, the Abbot teaches and leads by his word and example. He sees to it that all that is needed, from cowl to needle, is provided. As the father of the monastic family, his love and warmth of heart can best be exemplified by the words of the Abbot, St. Bernard, consoling the parents of a youthful postulant, 'Do not weep, do not cry. I shall be his brother and his sister – I shall be everything and I shall arrange for all his physical well-being and his spiritual development.'

St. Benedict regulated all in the monastery to establish and maintain a life of prayer, the ultimate goal pursued by the monk. The Benedictine, as well as the Cistercian monk, lives a communal life. With his brothers, he prays, works, has his meals and shares a dormitory. He speaks, however, only when it is absolutely necessary. The Carthusian monk, on the other hand, lives in solitude. Besides the nightly worship, the only contact he will have with his brothers takes place during the Sunday meal – eaten in silence – and the weekly walk. His silent life could be inspired by the Abbot Agatho, who it is said, for three years carried a stone in his mouth until he learned to be silent.

'Do not embrace soft living; love fasting', said St. Benedict. This instruction is reflected in the other orders too, but true humanity and care is always there in the monastic rule. The Usages of the Cistercian Monks says that 'the Abbot will see to it that the fare in the infirmary is more substantial than that served in the common refectory. The sick may take fish, eggs and dessert every day of the year.'

In every monastery there is much physical work to be done. All is dedicated to God and performed in obedience. 'As soon as the signal for work is given, we go to the auditorium where the Abbot assigns to each one his task. We tie up our robes modestly or put on work clothes – an apron, smock or overall, according to the nature of the work. We also change the shoes if necessary – we go to work in single file, following the Abbot' (Usages of the Cistercian Monks).

Every aspect of the monk's life is related to his primary quest for union with God. Even the admonishment of his Abbot is to be welcomed. 'Why do you correct your brother? Correct him from love of himself', said St. Augustine. 'The most usual penance is the recitation of some prayer. To do this we kneel before the principal table and recite the prayer silently, with the hands in the sleeves, unless the Abbot has told us to hold our arms extended in the form of a cross. Another penance is to take our soup on the floor. This is done by taking our soup sitting on a stool in the middle of the refectory. It can happen that for a grave fault a monk may be told to kiss the feet of the community. He begins with the Abbot, then goes to the Prior and then kisses the feet of all the monks and novices. He then salutes them' (Usages of the Cistercian Monks).

For the Carthusian monk, the cell is where his life is passed, in silence and obscurity. It is his dwelling place and it is his infirmary, should he fall ill. His meals are passed to him through a hatch in the wall near the entrance door of his cell. It is through this opening that he receives whatever else he may need from the outside – except a ladder to heaven. There is the continual wearing of the hair shirt and a black wooden cross hangs on the wall of a Carthusian's cell; as the final mark of obscurity, it will be placed over his grave without his name. The Carthusian Order is known as the 'Order of Iron'. There are thousands of Benedictine and Cistercian monks in monasteries throughout the world, whereas there are only a few hundred Carthusians.

It can be said that the Benedictine monasteries were islands of stability, and their inhabitants, almost alone, preserved learning in the West during the Dark Ages. The Cistercians, the White Monks, considered farming the chief occupation for monks; they led Europe in the development of agricultural techniques. The Carthusian has had the task – a divine task – of prayer and keeping guard over the spiritual welfare of nations, symbolizing the monk who stands between God and man.

✠ ✠ ✠

The Nun

by Dame Felicitas Corrigan OSB

✠   ✠   ✠

'BUT WHAT DO YOU DO ALL DAY?' Puzzled, awed, slightly querulous, the young and busy housewife obviously considered that between herself, burdened with many cares, and the carefree nun facing her in the monastic parlours, there was fixed a great gulf. With a glint of mischief in her eye, the nun obligingly took stock of her 'idle' day-to-day existence: 'Church, sacristies, chapter house, six long cloisters lined with windows, parlours, refectory, kitchens, laundry, bakehouse, libraries, loom room, printing house, infirmary, linen room, making and mending all our clothes, entertaining guests like you – just look around! Do you imagine that we have an army of fairies to do all the physical work involved?' The visitor laughed: the situation was saved.

All the same, it was a good question, and calls for a serious answer. Why on earth do some quite attractive young women – who presumably could easily find husbands – choose to reject God's world, to turn their backs on so much that is beautiful and the work of His hands? Among fervent Christians, many can readily appreciate a Mother Teresa of Calcutta, a missionary dispensing medicines under a blazing tropical sun, or a nun mothering motherless children: all these are the hands and feet of Christ going about His healing and apostolic ministry. But the so-called enclosed contemplatives – aren't they setting themselves up as some kind of esoteric elite, a mystical aristocracy that relegates the rank and file of Brother and Sister to the status of the second class?

There is no second class in the Christian Church. It was not to a chosen few that Christ our Lord addressed the words: 'Be perfect, as your heavenly Father is perfect.' Perfection is not graded. Each of us has a divine vocation, whether as husband or wife, parent, teacher, doctor, business tycoon, farmer, dock-labourer, monk or nun: what we do matters nothing; what we are matters everything. God has made hearts one by one, as the psalmist says, for with Him there is no mass production. Each human being reflects God according to temperament and personal call, some to the life of Martha, others to that of Mary. Underlying the question, 'What do you do all day?' is one left unsaid but much more probing. It is, 'What are you doing with God's gift of life? Throwing it away? To what purpose is this waste?' And the answer is simply: 'I'm giving my life back to Him in pure praise and thanksgiving, because God himself for his own secret purpose asks it of me.'

There can be no contradiction between the busy mother of children sweeping the floor or preparing soup for dinner and the nun, broom in hand or peeling vegetables for the midday meal. For those who live in the sacrament of the present moment, God is wholly and everywhere present. St. Teresa observed – and it applies both to housewife and nun – that many a time the woman who is hard at work is praying much more truly than the one who goes away by herself and meditates her head off.

Nevertheless there is a difference in the roles of parent and nun – they are complementary and need each other. If a young woman feels called to make a radical and exclusive renunciation of all subordinate goals, however lawful – and notably the joys of husband and home, she does so in the name and for the sake of the entire Church; at the same time, common sense points out that without fathers, mothers and family life there would be no potential priests, monks or nuns. So the score is fifty-fifty. On the one hand, Mary witnesses to the Absolute, to God's unchanging transcendence; on the other hand, Martha applies all her energies to the building on earth of the City of God.

There is an interesting divergence in the routes taken by nuns to reach their goal. The Benedictine, clad in sober black, would tell you that she is merely 'a Church-woman'. A probation of five years precedes the taking of vows; thenceforth her daily round from 5am to 10pm will be solemn liturgical and private prayer, work of any and all kinds – in the world today, enclosed nuns, like everyone else, have to earn their daily bread; the ravens no longer descend with loaves in their beaks as to the prophet Elijah. Nothing here dramatic or sensational.

The Poor Clares, barefooted beneath the rough brown tunic girded with threefold knotted cord, would inform you with great cheerfulness that the Poor Ladies, as they were first called, are wedded to poverty. They might possibly quote St. Clare's charge: 'For the love of the most sweet Child Jesus wrapped in swaddling bands, and of his holy Mother, I admonish, beseech and entreat my sisters that they always be clothed in poor garments.' The sway of Lady Poverty extends to every dimension of this austere life; no meat is ever taken, the nuns fast almost the whole year round, rise at midnight to chant Matins and spend an hour before the Blessed Sacrament before returning to rest at 2am only to rise again at 5am to face a busy day of prayer and work.

'In the heart of the Church, I will be love.' These words of St. Thérèse of Lisieux express in few words the specifically Carmelite vocation. Everything in a Carmelite's life is ordained to prayer, seen as an exchange of love. Not only does she spend at least an hour in silent prayer night and morning but, following the eremitical ideal of Carmelite tradition of the early 13th century, she sometimes retires for solitude and a deeper communion with God to the hermitages specially built in the grounds of the enclosure.

A contemplative nun is a powerful witness to God's kingdom, and joins St. Augustine in saying, 'This is my life: to praise You, my God.'

"This house is another
Heaven, if it be possible to
have Heaven on earth."

WAY OF PERFECTION

✢

*"At the gate of the monastery
let there be placed a wise old
man, who knows how to receive
and to give a message, and
whose maturity will prevent
him from straying about."*

BENEDICTINE RULE

✛

"The Portress should be of mature virtue and discreet, and should be of suitable age.
During the day she shall remain at the entry in a small open cell without a door. The Sisters shall not allow
anyone to enter the monastery before sunrise, nor to remain within after sunset."

WAY OF PERFECTION

‡

"When the physician comes, or the barber, or the confessor, or any other person whose presence is necessary, two Sisters must always accompany him."

WAY OF PERFECTION

"The monks come together in Chapter daily. It is in the Chapter that the monks assemble to deal with the business of the monastery. Everything that is said or done should remain secret."

CISTERCIAN RULE

⊹

"Once a week the Abbess is bound to assemble her Sisters at Chapter."

CARMELITE RULE

‑†‑

*"Every monastery has a
scriptorium where the monks
engage in intellectual work.
This room is well supplied with
all the books necessary for
Lectio Divina and the study
of the sacred sciences."*

CISTERCIAN RULE

✠

*"The library should provide
for an appropriate religious
culture, so that the Sisters may
learn to live their
contemplative vocation
with full knowledge of and
respect for truth."*

WAY OF PERFECTION

*"Only those books and
periodicals which do not
disturb their interior silence
are allowed. Medical books
are absolutely forbidden."*

CARTHUSIAN RULE

‡

*"We forbid also the same
Sisters to have, read, write
or cause to be written any
books that treat of the
dangerous and frivolous
pursuits of persons in
the world."*

WAY OF PERFECTION

✢

"The cell is his dwelling place and it is his infirmary, should he fall ill.

He sleeps on a straw pallet and wearing most of his clothing."

CISTERCIAN RULE

"*Those who are ill may lie on sacks filled with straw and have feather pillows for their heads...*
do not think of complaining about weaknesses and minor ailments from which women suffer,
for the Devil sometimes makes you imagine them. They come and go..."

WAY OF PERFECTION

✠

*"In his cell he shall occupy
himself in due order and
usefully in reading, writing,
reciting office, praying,
meditating, contemplating
and working."*

CARTHUSIAN RULE

✤

"All who profess this life shall be enclosed and have no leave or authority to go out, save only in case of imminent danger. Such dangers will be: fire, floods, destruction of buildings, terrors of war, military invasion..."

WAY OF PERFECTION

✠

"Let a senior monk be assigned to the novices, one who is skilled at winning

souls, to watch over them with particular attention."

BENEDICTINE RULE

✛

*"In the training of novices,
special attention is to be given
to Sacred Scriptures."*

WAY OF PERFECTION

✣

"Since we have freely left the world, we must take care that the world does not reach us.

We receive visits ordinarily only from our near relatives. These should not be too frequent."

CISTERCIAN RULE

✠

"The novices, like the professed Sisters, may receive visits; because we wish them to remain with us of their own free will,

and if for some reason they are unhappy and do not wish to stay, let them have the chance to make it known."

WAY OF PERFECTION

⊹

"We may affirm with St. Bernard that parents who
offer their son generously to the Lord do not lose him."

CISTERCIAN RULE

✠

"Oh, Sisters, for the love of God, try to realize what a great

favour the Lord has bestowed on us whom he has brought here."

WAY OF PERFECTION

✣

"The Abbot should provide all the necessary articles: cowl, tunic,
stockings, shoes, girdle, knife, pen, needle, handkerchief, tablets;
that all pretext of need may be taken away."

BENEDICTINE RULE

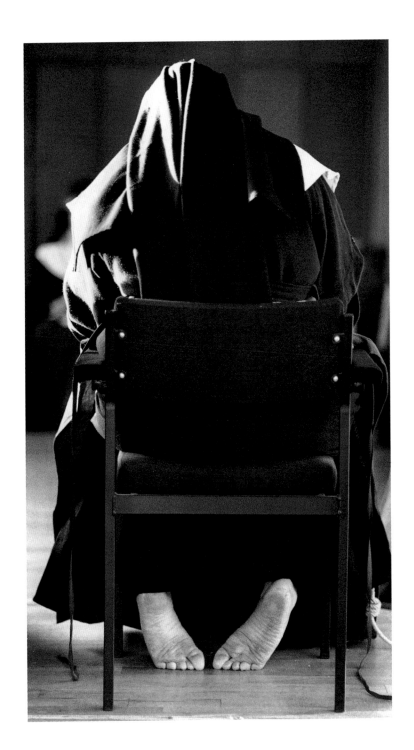

✝

"We declare that no Sister, whatever be her rank or office, may have woollen socks. Those who are able to do so go completely barefoot indoors.…."

POOR CLARES' RULE

✠

"Let them keep their hair short, so as not to waste time combing it. There must be no mirrors or anything fancy... all Sisters, without any distinction whatever, shall in all humility, modesty and piety... avoid singularity and vanity of all kinds."

WAY OF PERFECTION

☩

*"Three strokes of the great bell are tolled to summon the
ministers of the altar and to call the community to choir."*

CISTERCIAN RULE

✠

"As soon as the signal is heard, let them abandon whatever they may have in hand and hasten with the greatest speed, yet with seriousness."

BENEDICTINE RULE

✝

"At the first stroke of the bell, all the Sisters assemble in choir..."

WAY OF PERFECTION

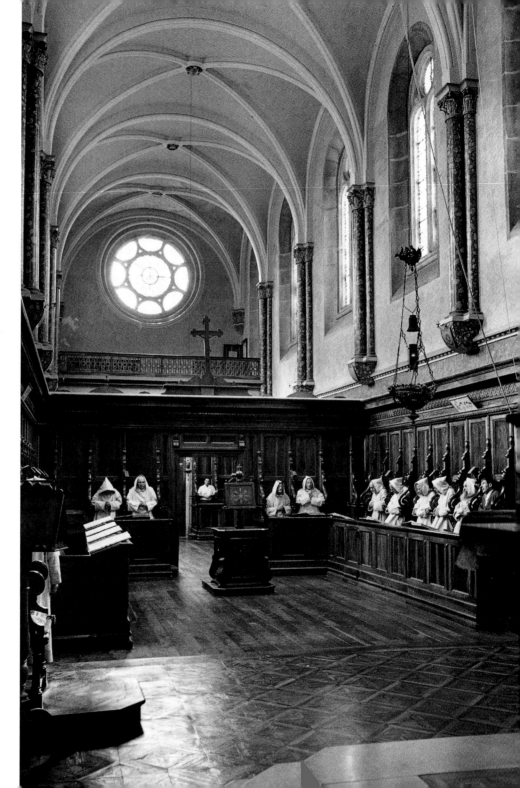

✝

"…to prepare their hearts for the Lord; there they shall remain without converse, murmur, laughter and without vain and idle looks, in silence and peace; and there they shall continue all together to the end."

WAY OF PERFECTION

✛

*"The beginning of our
Rule tells us to pray
without ceasing."*

WAY OF PERFECTION

✢

"If there are craftsmen in the monastery, let them practise their crafts with all humility."

BENEDICTINE RULE

☩

"Let us remember that we are subject to the common law of work which is the normal means of providing the necessities of life. We freely and gladly give ourselves to manual work and to the humbler and more toilsome household tasks of the monastery."

WAY OF PERFECTION

✠

"Even when alms are freely given to supply our needs, we should

have some suitable work by means of which we can assist others."

WAY OF PERFECTION

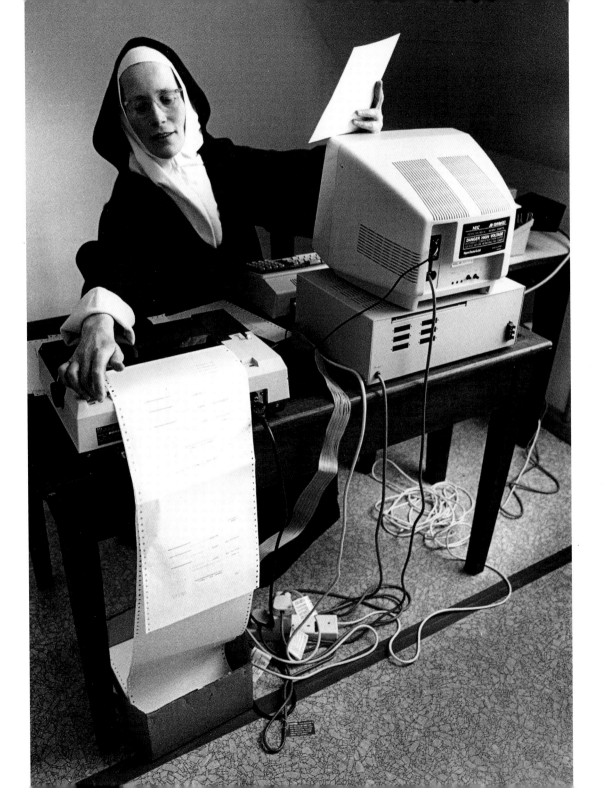

☩

The wines vary according to the availability of fruit: Apple; Damson; Elderberry; Folly (made from
vine prunings); Gooseberry; Grape (real wine); Lemon Verbena; Mead; Potato; Redcurrant & Rosepetal.
The wine is bottled for Christmas presents to friends of the community.

BENEDICTINE MONASTERY

⊹

"Then are they truly monks when they earn their living by the work of their hands."

BENEDICTINE RULE

✢

*"Do not think, my sisters, that because you do not go about trying to
please people in the world you will lack food. You will not, I assure you..."*

WAY OF PERFECTION

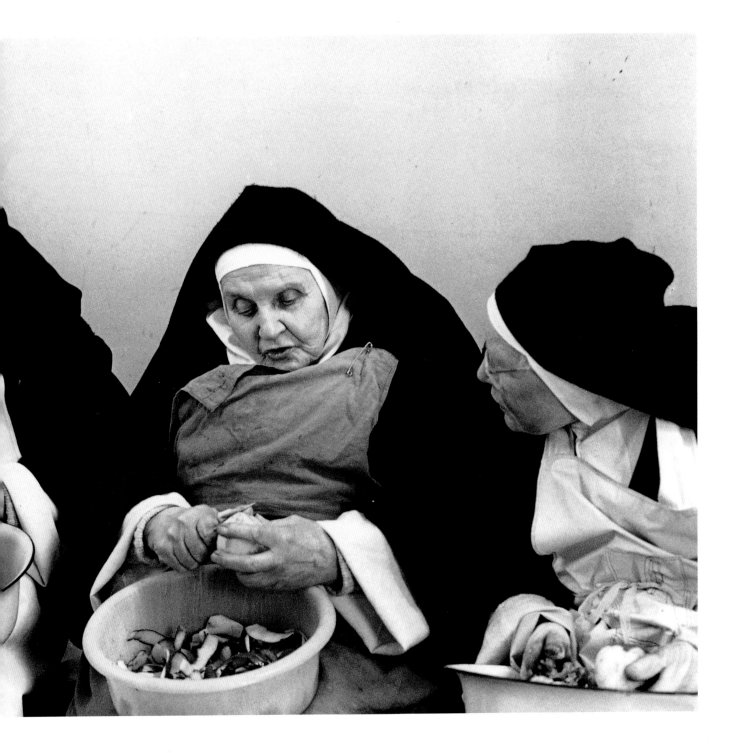

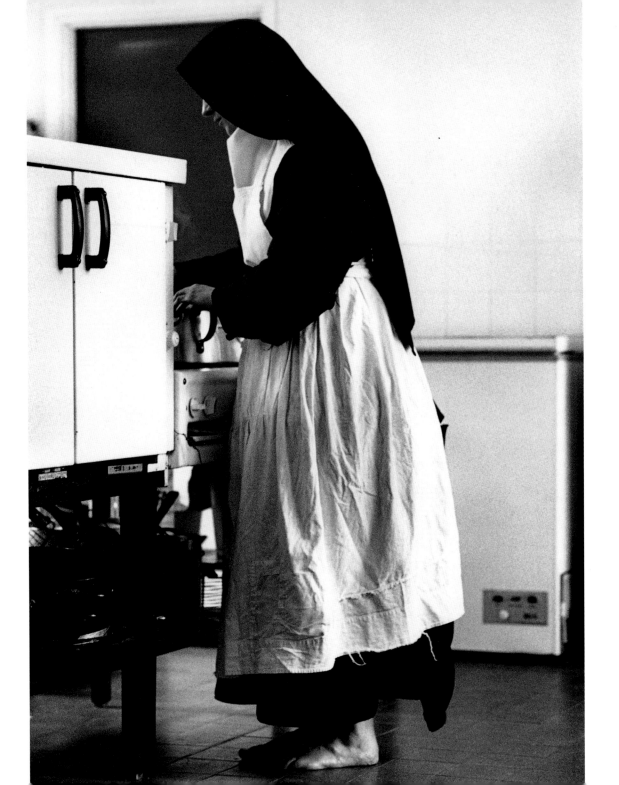

✛

"It is with some misgiving that we determine how much others should eat or drink.

Nevertheless, we believe that a hemina (½ pint) of wine a day is sufficient for each."

BENEDICTINE RULE

✛

"Choice wines and fish, which may indeed grace the banquets of the wealthy but which dishonour the mean Carthusian table, should be far removed from us."

CARTHUSIAN RULE

✝

"And if you are in the kitchen, our Lord moves among the pots and pans."

WAY OF PERFECTION

✢

"When dinner is over, the Mother Prioress may allow all the Sisters to talk of whatever they like, provided it be within the limits which a good religious order ought to observe: they must all have their distaffs with them."

WAY OF PERFECTION

✠

"In a sincere desire to share the joyful happiness of our hearts, we come together twice a day for recreation. Our Holy Mother wished us to do so and to make our common recreation moments of cheerful and unaffected happiness."

WAY OF PERFECTION

✛

"An old tradition says that the monk who is suffering should be treated in such a way that he will not regret the absence of his mother."

CISTERCIAN RULE

✠

"Our family spirit and love for each other should be evident in the love
and attention we lavish on sisters who are infirm through age or illness."

WAY OF PERFECTION

✝

"The monk attaches himself
until the end of his life to his
abbey and to the community
of which he becomes
a member."

CISTERCIAN RULE

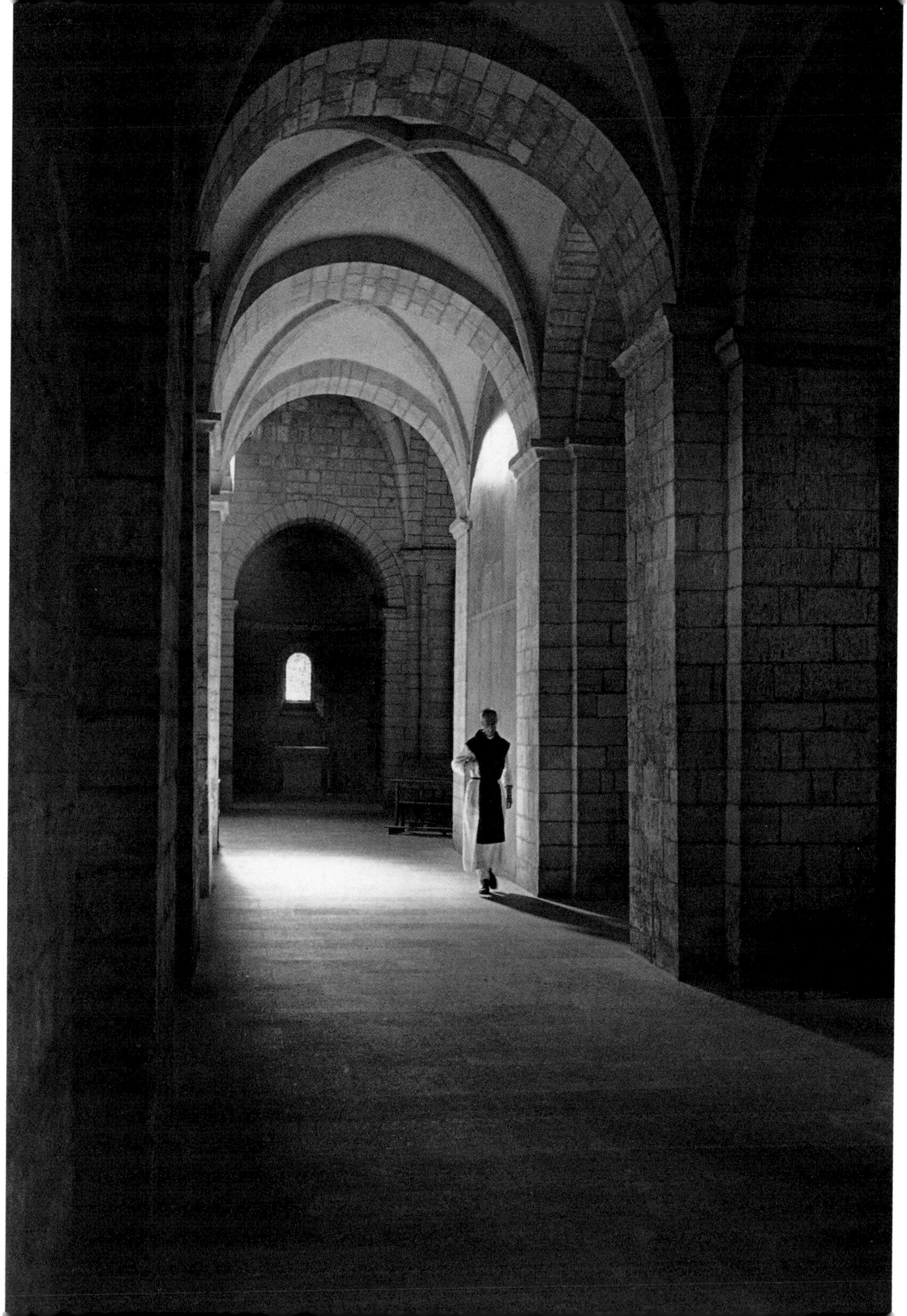

✠

"You may come from where you will in the world, even from its holiest shrines, but once arrived at the 'House of God and Gate of Heaven', you must become a saint, or you never will be one."

A CARTHUSIAN

The monks photographed in this book are Carthusians, Benedictines, Cistercians and Franciscans. The nuns are Carmelites, Benedictines and Poor Clares. The texts, excerpted from the following sources, are not necessarily related to the Orders of the monks and nuns shown in the photographs on the same page:

The Rule of St. Benedict
The Usages of the Cistercian Monks
The Carthusian Rule
Way of Perfection by St. Teresa of Avila
Poor Clares' Rule

Several of the photographs of the monks were previously published in *They Dwell in Monasteries* (Frederick Muller, UK; Seabury Press, USA 1982).

✠ ✠ ✠

11.7.01   Midwest $18.66 (21.95)   # 83032